Morning & Evening Affirmation Journal

Morning & Evening Affirmation Journal

Inspiring Prompts and Meditative Reflections
to Start and End Your Day

— NOELLE WHITTINGTON —

ROCKRIDGE
PRESS

Interior and Cover Designer: Monica Cheng
Art Producer: Sara Feinstein
Editor: Eun H. Jeong
Production Editor: Caroline Flanagan
Production Manager: Holly Haydash

Illustration used under license from Shutterstock.com
Author photo courtesy of Honey Head Films

Paperback ISBN: 978-1-63878-885-0
R0

THIS JOURNAL BELONGS TO

_____

Introduction

Hi, I'm Noelle Whittington, E-RYT 500 + YACEP. I'm a yoga and meditation teacher, mentor, musician, and spiritual empowerment coach. I began my career in 2005 as a fitness instructor. After leading yoga training for licensed studios and mentoring their staff since 2012, leading numerous international yoga retreats, and raising funds for nonprofit organizations, including the Homes of Hope India, I longed for a deeper, more personal connection to my students and clients. From this desire, I created Soul Alchemy Course—an online group coaching program and community incorporating the practices of yoga, Ayurveda, dance, music, and spirituality.

My intention with this journal is to give you, the reader, some practical, easy, and fun tools and practices to frame your day and help you find greater insight and create healthy habits to enhance your life. I am humbled by the power of the mind, which can be our greatest challenge or biggest ally. Luckily, we can harness this power through practices of present-moment awareness, like journaling, to help us navigate the ups and downs of life. With positive affirmations and self-reflection through morning and evening journaling, we can start and end our day with intention and reverence.

An affirmation is a short, positive statement that helps us overcome negative and self-sabotaging thoughts. My teachers would say that while all our thoughts are real, most are not true. According to the psychologists Matthew A. Killingsworth and Daniel T. Gilbert, we spend roughly half our waking hours thinking thoughts that are not based in the present moment, known as mind-wandering, and this can lead to stress, anxiety, and depression. However, we can change this behavior by focusing our mind on positive thoughts and mindfulness practices, like affirmations and journaling. These powerful practices can help us create peace and happiness, thereby increasing our quality of life.

Working with affirmations has helped me through many challenging times in my life. For example, I have a classical dance background, and during my adolescent years I developed some body dysmorphia. What I saw in the mirror was never good enough. I had to train my mind to accept my body as the healthy and strong vessel that it is. Every day, I used the mantra "You are beautiful" through stickers placed strategically in places that were part of my day—in my car, on the bathroom window—and eventually I began to feel more confident and secure in myself. Now in my forties, I love my body more than ever and am grateful every day for my health.

My hope is that you will find inspiration, as I did, from the simple yet powerful tools of affirmations and journaling to create a shift in mindset that can be life changing!

How to Use This Book

This journal is designed to help you start the day with positivity and end the day with self-reflection. Although each day has a theme, each morning and evening page stands alone, so you can enjoy the practices in the order that works for you. If you want, you can turn to a random page within the book and find chance inspiration rather than reading in a linear fashion. The format is "Choose your own adventure!"

Your journal offers the following elements:

Affirmations: These are positive statements that you can repeat to help you overcome negative thoughts. They can be used in any situation where you would like to see a positive change take place in your life.

Guided journal prompts: These are brief questions or statements that will encourage you to engage in self-reflection and write about what comes up from this contemplation. The morning journal prompts in this book will help you meet the day with gratitude and positivity, and the evening prompts will help you relax and let go at the end of the day.

Guidance to build your own affirmations: You will be provided the opportunity to create your own affirmations. This exercise can help you set an intention for the day. Setting an intention includes doing some self-reflection on what is important for the day and coming up with a statement that provides clear direction to help manifest a positive change in your life and focus on what's most important. I'll help you create your own positive statements that will encourage, uplift, and motivate you for the rest of the day. I'll invite you to think about how you can apply this to the day ahead and how it might inform your day's intention. The following are some guidelines on how to create your own affirmation:

- Make your affirmation short so it is clear and easy to remember.
- Focus on the affirmative rather than the negative. For example, instead of "I am so forgetful," try using "My brain is sharp and clear." See how it feels!
- Using "I" statements is most effective because they are personal and geared toward you. For example, "I am grateful for the abundance in my life" can be more powerful than "Gratitude creates abundance in life."
- Write your affirmations in the present tense as though you are experiencing what you want right now. This brings a powerful present-moment energy to your statement. "I am happy and grateful" is better than "I will be happy and grateful." Also, rather than adding a time frame ("In two months when I get that job, I will be successful"), focus on now ("I am successful and prosperous. New opportunities are coming my way!").

Calming practices called "wind-down practices": These are intended to help you reflect on your day and cultivate peace in the evening. They include exercises you can use to embrace more positivity and self-love in your life and to help you sleep well so you can wake up refreshed.

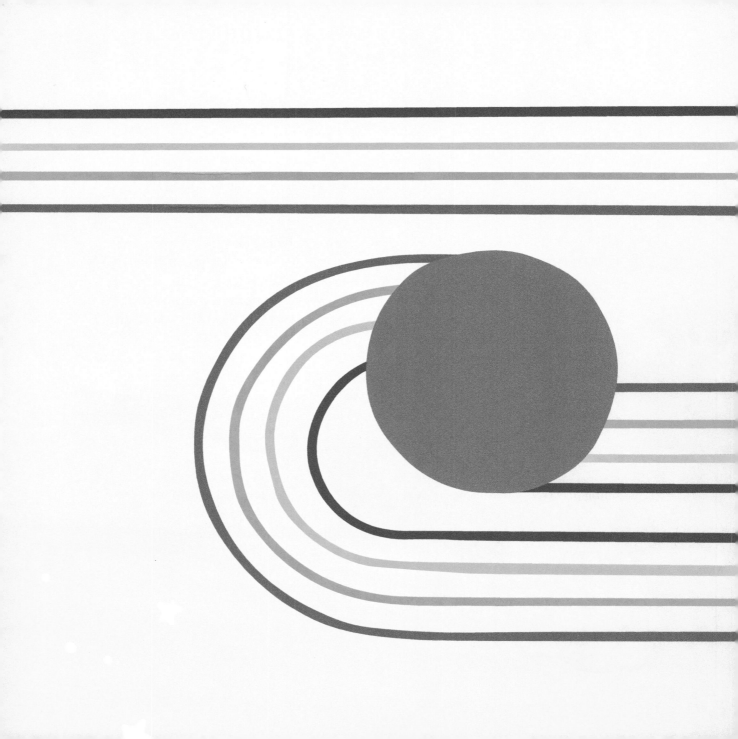

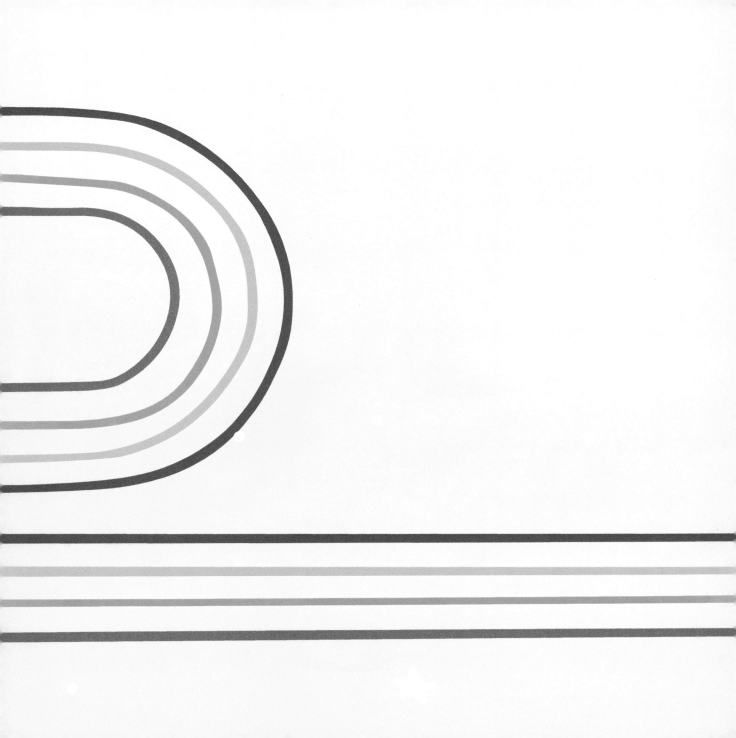

Meet the Day

MORNING AFFIRMATION

I am a magnet for abundance!

MORNING GUIDED PROMPT

What does *abundance* mean to you? How can you identify the abundance that is present in your life right now?

_____

_____

_____

_____

_____

_____

_____

_____

_____

Rest and Reflect

EVENING AFFIRMATION

I am grateful for all the things I have in my life.

WIND-DOWN PRACTICE

"Box Breath": Tension-Releasing Breathing Technique

1. Find a quiet, comfortable space and get into a supported position.

2. Close your eyes or focus your gaze on a nonmoving object.

3. Allow your belly to expand as you breathe in slowly through the nose for a count of 4. Then hold your breath in for 4 counts, keeping your jaw and shoulders relaxed. Exhale through the nose or mouth for a count of 4. Then hold the breath out for 4 counts, or fewer if necessary.

4. As you breathe, silently repeat the words "inhale" and "exhale."

5. Repeat this breathing for 3 to 5 minutes.

Date

Meet the Day

AFFIRMATION GUIDANCE

Habits are the building blocks that make up our life and help us achieve our goals. Instead of focusing on what is still to be done, think about the habits you have established that have gotten you this far.

I am creating my dream life by _____.

How might this inspire you in the day ahead?

_____

_____

_____

_____

_____

_____

_____

_____

_____

Rest and Reflect

EVENING GUIDED PROMPT

What is the nicest thing someone has ever said about you? How did it make you feel?

_____

_____

_____

_____

_____

_____

_____

_____

GRATITUDE PROMPT

I am grateful _____

_____ .

Meet the Day

MORNING AFFIRMATION

*Every day is a new chance for me—
the possibilities are endless!*

MORNING GUIDED PROMPT

Think of how your life was a year ago and reflect on all the positive changes you
have made.

_____

_____

_____

_____

_____

_____

_____

Rest and Reflect

EVENING AFFIRMATION

*Anything is possible because
I believe in myself and my dreams.*

WIND-DOWN PRACTICE

Alternate Nostril Breathing for Relaxation

1. Find a comfortable position in a quiet space. Reclining with a pillow under your knees can be very relaxing.

2. Using your right thumb to close your right nostril, breathe in slowly through the left nostril.

3. While releasing your right thumb, use your fourth finger to close your left nostril and exhale slowly through the right nostril.

4. Inhale through the right nostril.

5. Close the right with your thumb and exhale through the left.

6. Inhale through the left, close the left, and exhale through the right.

7. Repeat this cycle for a few minutes.

Meet the Day

AFFIRMATION GUIDANCE

An attitude of gratitude opens the door for more abundance to flow into your life. As you reflect on where you are in life today, take a moment to truly appreciate all the things you are thankful for.

Today, I am thankful for _____.

How might appreciation enhance your day today?

_____

_____

_____

_____

_____

_____

_____

Date _____

Rest and Reflect

EVENING GUIDED PROMPT

What are you taking for granted about your daily life that you can take time to appreciate now?

_____

_____

_____

_____

_____

_____

_____

_____

GRATITUDE PROMPT

I am grateful _____

_____.

Meet the Day

MORNING AFFIRMATION

I am open to the awesome opportunities coming my way.

MORNING GUIDED PROMPT

What is one healthy habit you could maintain each day that would have a positive effect on your life?

_____

_____

_____

_____

_____

_____

_____

_____

_____

Rest and Reflect

EVENING AFFIRMATION

*I am fully supported emotionally,
and I can reach out to ask for help anytime.*

WIND-DOWN PRACTICE

The 4-7-8 Breath: Reducing Anxiety for Restful Sleep

1. Silence your electronic devices and lie down in bed.

2. Empty your lungs of air.

3. Breathe in through the nose for 4 seconds, counting in your mind.

4. Hold the breath for 7 counts.

5. Exhale through the mouth forcefully for 8 counts, making a "whoosh" sound. Repeat the mantra "I release" in your mind as you exhale.

6. Repeat this breathing technique up to 4 times.

7. Switch to a soft inhale for 4 counts, hold the breath for 7 counts, and exhale for 8. Use the mantra "I am calm."

Meet the Day

AFFIRMATION GUIDANCE

Practicing present-moment awareness has many health benefits, including reduced stress and anxiety and improved overall quality of life. Being in the present moment also allows us to see the beauty all around us instead of worrying about what we can't see or control.

*My life is beautiful because*_____.

How will you enjoy the beautiful moments that today brings?

_____

_____

_____

_____

_____

_____

_____

_____

Rest and Reflect

EVENING GUIDED PROMPT

What accomplishments today are you proudest of, and why?

_____

_____

_____

_____

_____

_____

_____

_____

_____

GRATITUDE PROMPT

I am grateful _____

_____.

Meet the Day

MORNING AFFIRMATION

I release expectations and I accept myself exactly as I am today.

MORNING GUIDED PROMPT

What are you looking forward to today, and why?

_____

_____

_____

_____

_____

_____

_____

_____

Rest and Reflect

EVENING AFFIRMATION

I expect nothing and I appreciate everything.

WIND-DOWN PRACTICE

Visualization for Gratitude

1. Find a quiet area and sit in a comfortable position.

2. Close your eyes, take a deep breath, and visualize yourself in a beautiful landscape.

3. Engage all your senses, noticing what you see, hear, smell, touch, and taste. Spend a few minutes visualizing even the smallest details.

4. Before you open your eyes, offer gratitude for your imagination and the happiness it brings to your life.

Meet the Day

AFFIRMATION GUIDANCE

Practicing nonjudgment means releasing expectations. When we do this, we let go of what we thought would happen and accept and appreciate our life as it is. This release can help create a sense of ease.

I appreciate _____ *without judgment.*

How can you create a sense of ease today?

_____

_____

_____

_____

_____

_____

_____

_____

Rest and Reflect

EVENING GUIDED PROMPT

What is one important thing you have learned from a past or current relationship that helped you grow?

_____

_____

_____

_____

_____

_____

_____

_____

GRATITUDE PROMPT

I am grateful _____

_____ .

Meet the Day

MORNING AFFIRMATION

I attract happiness through my positive outlook.

MORNING GUIDED PROMPT

Take a moment to reflect on one of your many skills that brings you confidence.

_____

_____

_____

_____

_____

_____

_____

_____

_____

_____

Rest and Reflect

EVENING AFFIRMATION

My days are filled with joy and ease.

WIND-DOWN PRACTICE

Three Good Things

No matter what kind of day we have, there are many small things that go our way and there is always something to be grateful for. Spend a few minutes reflecting on the day until you think of three good things that happened.

1. _____
   _____

2. _____
   _____

3. _____
   _____

Meet the Day

AFFIRMATION GUIDANCE

Practicing contentment means seeing things as they are and appreciating the blessings we have. From this appreciation comes comfort and inner peace.

I find satisfaction in _____.

What can you do to find more satisfaction today?

_____

_____

_____

_____

_____

_____

_____

_____

Rest and Reflect

EVENING GUIDED PROMPT

What made you smile today? Try to remember the circumstances in detail.

_____

_____

_____

_____

_____

_____

_____

_____

_____

GRATITUDE PROMPT

I am grateful _____

_____.

Date

Meet the Day

MORNING AFFIRMATION

I am confident and secure in my body.

MORNING GUIDED PROMPT

Reflect on the ways you can show appreciation for all that your body does.

_____

_____

_____

_____

_____

_____

_____

_____

_____

_____

Rest and Reflect

EVENING AFFIRMATION

I am grateful for my body and all it does for me.

WIND-DOWN PRACTICE

Focusing on the Present for Serenity

Mindful awareness of the present moment can create a sense of calm and ease. Without dwelling on the past or worrying about the future, we recognize that in this moment all is well.

1. Find a comfortable sitting position in a quiet space.

2. Take a few deep breaths and close your eyes.

3. Notice your breath, softly moving in and out.

4. Feel the support of your seat, and notice any sounds you hear from outside or inside the room.

5. As you inhale, silently repeat "I am," and as you exhale, repeat "at peace."

Meet the Day

AFFIRMATION GUIDANCE

Security and confidence in our body comes from taking care of ourselves—by getting enough sleep, getting regular exercise, and eating healthy food. In this way we thank our body for all it does for us as we get stronger and healthier.

I love my body because _____.

What things can you do to practice self-care today?

_____

_____

_____

_____

_____

_____

_____

Rest and Reflect

EVENING GUIDED PROMPT

What would your closest friend say they love about you?

_____

_____

_____

_____

_____

_____

_____

_____

_____

GRATITUDE PROMPT

I am grateful _____

_____.

Meet the Day

MORNING AFFIRMATION

My mind is sharp and clear.

MORNING GUIDED PROMPT

Clarity of mind comes with the practice of being present in the moment. What is one way you could practice being more fully present today?

_____

_____

_____

_____

_____

_____

_____

_____

_____

Rest and Reflect

EVENING AFFIRMATION

I let go of every worry.

WIND-DOWN PRACTICE

Three-Part Breath for Sleep

Focusing the mind on an activity and a repeated phrase, called a mantra, can activate our "rest and digest" nervous system response, which has many benefits—including better sleep!

1. Get cozy in your bed and close your eyes.

2. Inhale into the lower lungs, expanding the belly. Continue into the rib cage, followed by the upper chest. Exhale, releasing the upper chest, rib cage, and belly.

3. As you inhale, repeat "I know I am breathing in," and as you exhale, repeat "I know I am breathing out."

4. Repeat for up to 10 minutes or until you feel sleepy.

Meet the Day

AFFIRMATION GUIDANCE

Mindfulness practices increase present-moment awareness, which in turn can improve focus and concentration. Mindfulness simply means paying attention and focusing all your awareness on the task at hand. Practicing mindfulness can help you find more satisfaction in the tasks you complete.

I choose to focus on _____.

How do the things you choose to focus on align with your values?

_____

_____

_____

_____

_____

_____

_____

_____

Rest and Reflect

EVENING GUIDED PROMPT

Taking time to wind down at the end of the day can lead to a more peaceful night. What are some peaceful practices you can incorporate into your evening?

_____

_____

_____

_____

_____

_____

_____

GRATITUDE PROMPT

I am grateful _____

_____ .

Meet the Day

MORNING AFFIRMATION

I welcome joy in my life.

MORNING GUIDED PROMPT

Music can be a source of inspiration and joy. What song helps you feel happy and energized, and why do you think it has this effect on you?

_____

_____

_____

_____

_____

_____

_____

_____

_____

Rest and Reflect

EVENING AFFIRMATION

I am relaxed and will sleep well tonight.

WIND-DOWN PRACTICE

Contemplation Meditation and Journaling

Contemplation can be very clarifying, bringing answers to questions on our mind. At the end of the day, take a moment to relax in a quiet space and enjoy some deep breaths. Ask yourself the question "What do I need to know now?" and wait for a few minutes, breathing slowly. Notice information coming in from all your senses. Don't worry about forcing an answer to come in the form of a thought—the answer might come later, in a different way. Journal about whatever came up for you.

_____

_____

_____

_____

_____

Meet the Day

AFFIRMATION GUIDANCE

Along with the multiple health benefits we gain from bringing laughter into our life, laughing just makes us feel good. Laughter eases worry, stress, and anxiety and can give us a more positive outlook on life.

I am delighted by _____.

When was the last time you laughed uncontrollably? Relive the memory.

_____

_____

_____

_____

_____

_____

_____

Date _____

Rest and Reflect

EVENING GUIDED PROMPT

*Take some time to reflect on three things
that delighted you today.*

_____

_____

_____

_____

_____

_____

GRATITUDE PROMPT

I am grateful _____

_____ .

Meet the Day

MORNING AFFIRMATION

Joy infuses my day—I am happy!

MORNING GUIDED PROMPT

Movement and exercise can bring many health benefits, including a better mood. How can you infuse more movement into your week?

_____

_____

_____

_____

_____

_____

_____

_____

_____

Rest and Reflect

EVENING AFFIRMATION

I choose to release all that no longer serve me.

WIND-DOWN PRACTICE

Intention and Mantras for Manifestation

1. Find a quiet, relaxing space and settle into a comfortable position.

2. Close your eyes, take a few deep breaths, and reflect on what is important to you.

3. Create a short statement about something you would like to manifest. Use the present tense, as if it is already happening; for example, "Because my health is important, I exercise three times a week."

4. As you focus on your breath, repeat the mantra for a few minutes. When you are done, write down the mantra and place it where you can see it tomorrow.

Meet the Day

AFFIRMATION GUIDANCE

By practicing self-reflection, we can discover and clarify what is most important to us. Knowing our top needs and values can help us in making decisions. When we say yes to things based on this wisdom, our life will be even more fulfilling.

_____ *is really important to me.*

How will knowing what is important to you inspire your day?

_____

_____

_____

_____

_____

_____

_____

Rest and Reflect

EVENING GUIDED PROMPT

Take some time to reflect on how your activities today reflected what is most important to you.

_____

_____

_____

_____

_____

_____

_____

_____

GRATITUDE PROMPT

I am grateful _____

_____ .

Meet the Day

MORNING AFFIRMATION

I am motivated and inspired.

MORNING GUIDED PROMPT

Call to mind someone you look up to. How do they inspire you?

_____

_____

_____

_____

_____

_____

_____

_____

_____

_____

Rest and Reflect

EVENING AFFIRMATION

*I take pride in the big and small things
I have accomplished in my life.*

WIND-DOWN PRACTICE

Candle Gazing Meditation

1. Light a candle in a quiet, low-lit space and take a comfortable seat.

2. Take deep, relaxing breaths while gazing at the candle.

3. After a few breaths, close your eyes and focus on the image of the candle in your mind. When the image fades away, open your eyes and gaze at the candle again.

4. Repeat this process for a few minutes.

5. If you like, journal for a few minutes on anything that arose from your meditation.

_____

_____

Meet the Day

AFFIRMATION GUIDANCE

Look back on your life to this point, then take a moment to recognize and celebrate your accomplishments. Perhaps think about where you were in your life only one short year ago, and notice how far you have come.

I am proud of _____.

How might you celebrate yourself today?

_____

_____

_____

_____

_____

_____

_____

_____

Rest and Reflect

EVENING GUIDED PROMPT

How can you be more loving and gentle with yourself?

_____

_____

_____

_____

_____

_____

_____

_____

_____

GRATITUDE PROMPT

I am grateful _____

_____.

Meet the Day

MORNING AFFIRMATION

*My body is a temple. I will treat it
with care and respect.*

MORNING GUIDED PROMPT

How will you care for your whole being today—physically, mentally, and emotionally?

_____

_____

_____

_____

_____

_____

_____

_____

Rest and Reflect

EVENING AFFIRMATION

Today was a gift and tomorrow will be even better.

WIND-DOWN PRACTICE

Self-Care Rituals: Oil Massage

Oil massage is not only hydrating for the skin, it can also relieve muscular tension and lubricate the joints. Use any oil that is unrefined, organic, and untoasted, like sesame or coconut oil. Put some of the oil in your palms to warm it up, and begin with long strokes down the bones and a circular motion around the joints. Take your time. If you like, take a warm shower or bath afterward without washing off the oil with soap—the heat will allow the oil to absorb into your skin. Sleep well!

Meet the Day

AFFIRMATION GUIDANCE

We can create a sense of ease in our life by understanding that there will be easy days and challenging days. By trusting that everything changes, we can appreciate the learning and growth, and look forward to thriving again.

I have faith in myself because _____.

How might you reflect on your personal growth over the years?

_____

_____

_____

_____

_____

_____

_____

Rest and Reflect

EVENING GUIDED PROMPT

Do you have a dream you have never shared with anyone? What is the dream?

_____

_____

_____

_____

_____

_____

_____

_____

GRATITUDE PROMPT

I am grateful _____

_____.

Meet the Day

MORNING AFFIRMATION

I show up as my authentic self—I love who I am!

MORNING GUIDED PROMPT

What makes you feel most authentic? Name three values that you hold close and shape who you are.

_____

_____

_____

_____

_____

_____

_____

_____

Rest and Reflect

EVENING AFFIRMATION

*I surround myself with a community
who appreciates me.*

WIND-DOWN PRACTICE

Self-Care Rituals: Reading

At the end of a long day, it can be comforting to curl up in bed with a good book, especially since many of us are on our computers and devices all day working. Set your alarm for the morning, then silence your electronics. Pour yourself a cup of tea, light a candle, grab a favorite book, and settle into bed. Read until you feel sleepy. Resist the urge to look at your phone again before you turn out the light. Good night!

Meet the Day

AFFIRMATION GUIDANCE

Your community is filled with inspiring, loving people whom you can count on. They allow you to show up as your authentic self, and they appreciate you for who you truly are.

I am supported by _____.

How might you surround yourself with a support community today?

_____

_____

_____

_____

_____

_____

_____

Rest and Reflect

EVENING GUIDED PROMPT

Reflect on someone in your life who recently showed up to support you. What did they do, and how did it make you feel?

_____

_____

_____

_____

_____

_____

_____

GRATITUDE PROMPT

I am grateful _____

_____.

Meet the Day

MORNING AFFIRMATION

I am inspired by the natural world.

MORNING GUIDED PROMPT

You are a multifaceted being. What are the ways you can embrace every part of yourself?

_____

_____

_____

_____

_____

_____

_____

_____

_____

_____

Date

Rest and Reflect

EVENING AFFIRMATION

*I am surrounded by beauty,
and I cultivate that within myself.*

WIND-DOWN PRACTICE

Ninety-Ninety: Relaxation Posture

It can be relaxing at the end of a long day to lie down and prop up the legs. This gentle inversion takes the pressure off your back, hips, legs, and feet and is very calming for the cardiovascular and nervous systems.

1. Lie down on the floor in front of a chair or a couch.

2. Prop up your legs on the couch or chair so that your hips and knees are bent at a 90-degree angle, or at whatever angle is most comfortable for you without putting any strain on your back or joints.

3. Take deep breaths while you hold this position for a few minutes.

Meet the Day

AFFIRMATION GUIDANCE

The natural world is filled with inspiring beauty. We are a part of nature. In appreciating nature, we can connect more deeply with ourselves.

I am like nature, filled with _____.

How will you infuse your day with nature?

_____

_____

_____

_____

_____

_____

_____

_____

Rest and Reflect

EVENING GUIDED PROMPT

What is one of your favorite aspects of nature, and why?

_____

_____

_____

_____

_____

_____

_____

_____

_____

GRATITUDE PROMPT

I am grateful _____

_____ .

Meet the Day

MORNING AFFIRMATION

*Today I will care for all parts of myself—
my physical body, my mind,
my energy, and my spirit.*

MORNING GUIDED PROMPT

We attract abundance by accepting things as they are and allowing rather than forcing things to happen. Continuing to honor a commitment that no longer serves us can limit our growth. What can you let go of to make space for other things that are in alignment with you?

_____

_____

_____

_____

_____

Rest and Reflect

EVENING AFFIRMATION

*I rest easily tonight in deep connection
with all parts of myself.*

WIND-DOWN PRACTICE

Whole Being Meditation

1. Find a comfortable position in a quiet place.

2. Close your eyes and breathe deeply.

3. Bring your awareness to your physical body, noticing all the sensations. Breathe into any tension you have.

4. Bring your awareness to your mind. Notice its activity, as you let go of trying to change it.

5. Notice your energy level and how the energy is flowing through your body. Breathe in such a way that feels balancing to your body.

6. Check in with your spirit, the center of your being. Offer gratitude.

Date _____

Meet the Day

AFFIRMATION GUIDANCE

When we integrate all aspects of ourselves, we are practicing full self-care. When we tend to the needs of our body, mind, energy, and spirit, we can truly thrive.

I care for my whole self by _____.

How will you connect more deeply with all aspects of yourself today?

_____

_____

_____

_____

_____

_____

_____

_____

Rest and Reflect

EVENING GUIDED PROMPT

Recall a time when you felt deeply connected to yourself and the universe. Describe the memory.

_____

_____

_____

_____

_____

_____

_____

_____

GRATITUDE PROMPT

I am grateful _____

_____ .

Meet the Day

MORNING AFFIRMATION

*I am thoughtful about my words,
and I practice compassionate communication.*

MORNING GUIDED PROMPT

Compassionate communication means that we consider the needs of the other person when making a request, while being honest about our own personal experience, in an effort to compromise. This cultivates a deeper connection to others. What clear request could you make of a loved one today?

_____

_____

_____

_____

_____

_____

Rest and Reflect

EVENING AFFIRMATION

I am grateful for my ability to speak up for myself because my feelings and needs matter.

WIND-DOWN PRACTICE

Coloring: An Artistic Meditation

According to a 2005 study by Curry and Kasser, coloring can help refocus our attention, promoting a sense of calm. Grab a pencil, markers, crayons, or whatever you have around the house and start doodling. Your inner child will remember this creative activity. If you like, create a little doodle here:

Meet the Day

AFFIRMATION GUIDANCE

You receive important information from your mind and your intuition all the time. While your thoughts are real, not all are true. Your mind is trying to keep you safe, but often it can be your biggest critic. Check in with yourself often to make sure you are not being misguided by your thoughts.

I am guided by _____.

How do you recognize your inner guidance, or intuition?

_____

_____

_____

_____

_____

_____

_____

Rest and Reflect

EVENING GUIDED PROMPT

Think of a time when you followed your intuition. What came from trusting your inner guide?

_____

_____

_____

_____

_____

_____

_____

_____

GRATITUDE PROMPT

I am grateful _____

_____.

Meet the Day

MORNING AFFIRMATION

I create healthy habits and remain committed to them through self-discipline.

MORNING GUIDED PROMPT

Self-discipline is a form of self-care. Spending our energy and time doing what is most important to us can lead to a happier, more productive life. What do you want to spend more time doing?

_____

_____

_____

_____

_____

_____

Rest and Reflect

EVENING AFFIRMATION

I am fully committed to my own wellness.

WIND-DOWN PRACTICE

Emotional Check-In

At the end of the day, it can be helpful to check in on our feelings and needs. Take a moment now to notice how you felt throughout the day. If you like, ask yourself these questions:

1. How am I feeling now?

_____

_____

2. What are my needs and what compassionate requests can I make of my loved ones to help me meet those needs?

_____

_____

Meet the Day

AFFIRMATION GUIDANCE

Finding rhythms in our life starts with creating healthy habits. By committing to wellness, we can make each day a new opportunity for growth.

I treat myself well by honoring the habit of _____.

Today is a new day. How will you spend it?

_____

_____

_____

_____

_____

_____

_____

_____

_____

Date

Rest and Reflect

EVENING GUIDED PROMPT

We have all likely heard the saying "Be careful what you wish for." What is something unexpected you have gained or received that you are grateful for?

_____

_____

_____

_____

_____

_____

_____

_____

GRATITUDE PROMPT

I am grateful _____

_____.

Meet the Day

MORNING AFFIRMATION

When my mind wanders into self-judgment, I bring it back to appreciation by focusing on my breath.

MORNING GUIDED PROMPT

What is something about yourself that you are learning to appreciate?

_____

_____

_____

_____

_____

_____

_____

Rest and Reflect

EVENING AFFIRMATION

I practice loving observation of my judgment with gratitude for my awareness and self-compassion.

WIND-DOWN PRACTICE

Being Gentle with Yourself

Take a moment to slow down and breathe. Find a comfortable position in a quiet place. If you like, light a candle and put on some soft music. Rub your hands together to warm them up and fill them with good energy. Place your hands on your heart and take 3 deep, cleansing breaths. Repeat the words "I am enough, I do enough, and I have enough" for a few minutes while breathing deeply. Close this practice with a moment of gratitude.

Meet the Day

AFFIRMATION GUIDANCE

Our thinking mind is our caretaker. It cares deeply about us and wants to keep us safe, but to do so, it may bring up past experiences that create limiting beliefs about ourselves. We can be grateful for those thoughts but also move past them by practicing self-compassion.

I practice self-compassion by _____.

How can this shift in perspective inform your day?

_____

_____

_____

_____

_____

_____

_____

_____

Rest and Reflect

EVENING GUIDED PROMPT

Reflect on something you have overcome that you are proud of. What wisdom have you gained because of this challenge? Shower yourself with love and admiration.

_____

_____

_____

_____

_____

_____

_____

_____

GRATITUDE PROMPT

I am grateful _____

_____.

Meet the Day

MORNING AFFIRMATION

I attract good people into my life.

MORNING GUIDED PROMPT

What are three important values you share with the people who are closest to you? How does this inspire you?

_____

_____

_____

_____

_____

_____

_____

_____

_____

Rest and Reflect

EVENING AFFIRMATION

I have an abundance of love in my life.

WIND-DOWN PRACTICE

Free-Form Movement

Dancing can be a joyous, inspiring, and therapeutic practice.

At the end of the day, play some of your favorite music and let your body move freely. You can move in any way that is comfortable for you, or you can follow the steps below.

Loosen up. Start with swinging your arms as you walk around the room. Then, stand in one place and move your torso in a circle. Shake your hands and shoulders. Roll your neck. All the while, take big deep breaths in and exhale through your mouth with a sigh. When you feel tired, lie down on your back and stretch your legs and hips to end the practice.

Meet the Day

AFFIRMATION GUIDANCE

By being a good person and focusing on treating others well, we can attract good people into our life who uplift and inspire us. These people can remind us that we have a great deal of love in our life already.

I attract _____.

How might this thought shape your intention for the day?

_____

_____

_____

_____

_____

_____

_____

_____

Date _____

Rest and Reflect

EVENING GUIDED PROMPT

Think about a friend you can always count on, and reflect on the qualities of a good friend that they exhibit. How does this inspire you?

_____

_____

_____

_____

_____

_____

_____

_____

GRATITUDE PROMPT

I am grateful _____

_____.

Meet the Day

MORNING AFFIRMATION

I am wealthy and prosperous—
I have so many blessings!

MORNING GUIDED PROMPT

Call to mind a recent blessing of prosperity you have received in your life. Relive the feelings that came with this gift.

_____

_____

_____

_____

_____

_____

_____

Rest and Reflect

EVENING AFFIRMATION

*I am calm and at ease knowing prosperity
is always flowing my way.*

WIND-DOWN PRACTICE

Calming Spinal Twists

Stretching your back with a twist at the end of the day can be very calming and can aid in healthy digestion.

1. Find a comfortable space to lie on your back on the floor.

2. Hug your knees into your chest and rock from side to side, taking deep breaths.

3. Release your legs to the floor on the left, keeping them bent, and extend both arms out in a T position.

4. Hold this position as you take 4 deep breaths.

5. Lift your legs back to the center, release them on the right side, and extend both arms out in a T position.

6. Hold this position as you take 4 deep breaths.

7. Return your legs to center and rest.

Meet the Day

AFFIRMATION GUIDANCE

Prosperity is the active energy of abundance. When you become aware of, and grateful for, the abundance already in your life, you may find that more blessings flow your way.

I am blessed by _____.

How might this bring happiness into your life today?

_____

_____

_____

_____

_____

_____

_____

_____

Rest and Reflect

EVENING GUIDED PROMPT

With a spirit of gratitude and positivity, we can always find something good about our day. What brought you joy today?

_____

_____

_____

_____

_____

_____

_____

_____

GRATITUDE PROMPT

I am grateful _____

_____.

Meet the Day

MORNING AFFIRMATION

*I can do anything because I believe
in myself and my abilities.*

MORNING GUIDED PROMPT

Do you have a big dream for your life right now? What will your life look like when you achieve this goal?

_____

_____

_____

_____

_____

_____

_____

_____

Rest and Reflect

EVENING AFFIRMATION

I understand that rest is productive.

WIND-DOWN PRACTICE

Temple and Jaw Massage

Sometimes we hold tension in our temples and jaw without realizing it. For a relaxing end to the day, give yourself a facial massage.

1. Start by taking a few deep breaths, inhaling and exhaling slowly through your mouth.

2. Stretch your jaw muscles by opening and closing your mouth.

3. Run your tongue over your teeth and swallow.

4. Rub your face gently using your index and middle finger in a circular motion around the jaw hinge, working your way up to the temples beside the eyes. Take relaxing breaths all the while. Enjoy!

Meet the Day

AFFIRMATION GUIDANCE

Life can get very busy. When we allow ourselves to rest, inspiration and creativity are reenergized. Rest is vital for productivity and allows for a healthy growth mindset.

I am balanced because _____.

How can you incorporate more rest and creativity into your life?

_____

_____

_____

_____

_____

_____

_____

_____

_____

Rest and Reflect

EVENING GUIDED PROMPT

Self-care rituals in the evening can help us wind down from the day and can help balance the stimulation we have experienced. What self-care ritual can you incorporate into your nightly routine?

_____

_____

_____

_____

_____

_____

_____

_____

GRATITUDE PROMPT

I am grateful _____

_____ .

Date

Meet the Day

MORNING AFFIRMATION

I am courageous and honest—
with myself and everyone in my life.

MORNING GUIDED PROMPT

Acknowledging others' feelings and having our own feelings acknowledged is a balance within compassionate communication. Considering others so that they might also consider us is important. Think of a situation where you could be honest with someone in your life and how honesty could deepen your connection.

_____

_____

_____

_____

_____

_____

Rest and Reflect

EVENING AFFIRMATION

I am grateful for deep connections with those who share my values.

WIND-DOWN PRACTICE

Letting Go of the Day with Simple Movement

1. Begin in a quiet space in a comfortable seated position.

2. Take 3 deep breaths, exhaling slowly through your mouth.

3. Gently roll your neck and turn your head from side to side.

4. Roll your shoulders.

5. Gently and slowly move your spine in all directions, keeping your seat planted on the ground or on your chair.

6. End the practice by lying on your back and breathing for a few minutes.

Meet the Day

AFFIRMATION GUIDANCE

Conversations with other people who share your interests can be inspiring and invigorating. Sharing dialogue with colleagues or loved ones may bring about new perspectives that you might not have considered otherwise. Every day can be a new chance for learning and growth.

I share my thoughts _____.

How might this pique your curiosity today?

_____

_____

_____

_____

_____

_____

_____

_____

Rest and Reflect

EVENING GUIDED PROMPT

Recall a time when a conversation with a friend helped you gain a new perspective on a subject. What did you discuss and how did your viewpoint evolve?

_____

_____

_____

_____

_____

_____

_____

_____

GRATITUDE PROMPT

I am grateful _____

_____.

Date

Meet the Day

MORNING AFFIRMATION

I love learning something new every day.

MORNING GUIDED PROMPT

If you could go anywhere in the world, where would you go? What would you like to see?

_____

_____

_____

_____

_____

_____

_____

_____

_____

_____

Rest and Reflect

EVENING AFFIRMATION

*I look forward to trying new things,
meeting new people, and seeing new places.*

WIND-DOWN PRACTICE

Positive Vibrations

The sound of our own voice can be a powerful tool in connecting deeply with ourselves. Singing or even humming can help us express ourselves in a therapeutic way. Did you know that when a group of people sing together, their heart rates sync up?

Take a moment to check in with yourself. How would you like to feel right now? Choose a song that creates this mood for you, and hum or sing along. Release any judgment about the sound of your voice and try to stay connected to the joy of the practice itself.

Meet the Day

AFFIRMATION GUIDANCE

According to the National Institutes of Health's ACTIVE study, learning new things creates new neural pathways in the brain, which helps maintain cognitive function. Learning new things is also fun!

Every day, I learn _____.

What are some things you have always wanted to learn?

_____

_____

_____

_____

_____

_____

_____

Rest and Reflect

EVENING GUIDED PROMPT

Reflect on something you learned that was challenging and is now a big part of your life. Celebrate yourself for your commitment to growth.

_____

_____

_____

_____

_____

_____

_____

GRATITUDE PROMPT

I am grateful _____

_____ .

Meet the Day

MORNING AFFIRMATION

I am grateful for my ability to choose what I want to do in my life. I am free!

MORNING GUIDED PROMPT

What choices could you make in your life today that would bring a sense of ease?

_____

_____

_____

_____

_____

_____

_____

_____

Rest and Reflect

EVENING AFFIRMATION

I am creating the life of my dreams, one day at a time.

WIND-DOWN PRACTICE

Dream Life Visualization

To create the life of our dreams, we first need to get clear on what we want.

1. Find a comfortable position in a quiet place.

2. Close your eyes and enjoy a few deep breaths.

3. Visualize what your dream life would be like. Notice information from all your senses—sound, touch, taste, sight, and smell. Notice how you feel.

4. Notice where you are in your dream life, who is with you, and the activities you are doing.

5. Journal about your experience.

_____

_____

_____

Date

Meet the Day

AFFIRMATION GUIDANCE

Recall the last time you felt free. Take a moment to consider the activities, people, and places that help you feel a sense of freedom and joy. Revel in these sweet memories.

I feel most free when _____.

How can you incorporate more of this freedom into your life today?

_____

_____

_____

_____

_____

_____

_____

_____

_____

Rest and Reflect

EVENING GUIDED PROMPT

What activities or people are daily sources of positivity? Allow yourself a sense of gratitude for their presence in your life.

_____

_____

_____

_____

_____

_____

_____

_____

GRATITUDE PROMPT

I am grateful _____

_____.

Meet the Day

MORNING AFFIRMATION

I surround myself with objects and hobbies I enjoy.

MORNING GUIDED PROMPT

Music has a healing vibrational quality. Each of the five elements (earth, water, fire, air, and space) is represented by a type of sound. We are made up of the elements and therefore drawn to certain vibrations. What sounds inspire you the most, and why?

Rest and Reflect

EVENING AFFIRMATION

I deserve rest and care.

WIND-DOWN PRACTICE

Calming Fingertip Mindfulness Exercise

It is common to have to deal with excess energy, in the body and the mind. Often, our thoughts take over and can stress us out. Bring your mind back to a neutral point with this simple exercise.

1. Find a comfortable position and breathe deeply and slowly.

2. With your arms relaxed, touch the thumb to each finger pad while counting. Inhale and touch each finger while counting up to 4.

3. Continue counting to 8 as you exhale.

4. Repeat for a few minutes until you feel relaxed.

Meet the Day

AFFIRMATION GUIDANCE

Taking a break during the workday is part of a healthy, balanced lifestyle. Using essential oils, doing yoga, or taking a walk can be helpful aids for a peaceful day.

I allow myself to _____.

Reflect on how it feels to take a break during your day.

_____

_____

_____

_____

_____

_____

_____

_____

Rest and Reflect

EVENING GUIDED PROMPT

Reflect on a break you took today and how it made you feel. You deserve time to rest and reflect. Congratulate yourself on a well-balanced day.

_____

_____

_____

_____

_____

_____

_____

_____

GRATITUDE PROMPT

I am grateful _____

_____.

Meet the Day

MORNING AFFIRMATION

Exercise makes me feel good,
so I move my body every day.

MORNING GUIDED PROMPT

What is one of your favorite forms of exercise, and why? How can you incorporate it into your regular routine?

_____

_____

_____

_____

_____

_____

_____

_____

Rest and Reflect

EVENING AFFIRMATION

*I go to sleep satisfied, knowing that I made
the most of this precious day.*

WIND-DOWN PRACTICE

Intuitive Drawing

Much like coloring, drawing can be a great way to relax your body and mind while expressing yourself. Grab a piece of paper and something to draw with.

1. Close your eyes and take a deep breath.

2. Open your eyes and draw a tree.

3. Close your eyes again, take a deep breath, and ask yourself, "What am I most grateful for?"

4. Open your eyes and draw what you are grateful for as fruits or flowers on the tree.

5. Add anything else you like to your gratitude tree.

Meet the Day

AFFIRMATION GUIDANCE

Present-moment awareness through meditation has numerous health benefits, including clarity in decision-making. Taking time to focus on your breath can aid in bringing more insight to your day.

In this moment, _____ *is most important.*

How could this inform your choices today?

_____

_____

_____

_____

_____

_____

_____

_____

Rest and Reflect

EVENING GUIDED PROMPT

As you relax at the end of the day, take a moment to connect with yourself. Ask yourself, "What is most important right now?" Journal on what comes up for you.

_____

_____

_____

_____

_____

_____

_____

GRATITUDE PROMPT

I am grateful _____

_____.

Meet the Day

MORNING AFFIRMATION

My heart speaks to me, and I trust its guidance.

MORNING GUIDED PROMPT

Recall a time when you followed your heart's guidance. Where did it lead?

_____

_____

_____

_____

_____

_____

_____

_____

_____

_____

_____

Rest and Reflect

EVENING AFFIRMATION

I deserve to live a life of total fulfillment.

WIND-DOWN PRACTICE

Love Note to Your Self

Set the stage for a romantic night this evening with your one true love—you! Light a candle, perhaps, or some incense to set the mood. Grab a pen and settle into a comfortable space. Take a few deep breaths and focus on your heart. Journal on the following:

1. What do you love about your body? How about your character?

_____

_____

2. Write something you have accomplished that you are proud of.

_____

_____

Meet the Day

AFFIRMATION GUIDANCE

According to Ayurveda (the ancient system of holistic wellness), the four objectives of life are purpose, wealth/abundance, enjoyment, and liberation. In Western culture we often view enjoyment as a luxury, even though pleasure is actually essential for total wellness and longevity.

I enjoy _____.

How will you enjoy life more today?

_____

_____

_____

_____

_____

_____

_____

_____

Rest and Reflect

EVENING GUIDED PROMPT

Contemplating what you desire is the first step to manifestation. If you were granted three wishes, what would they be?

_____

_____

_____

_____

_____

_____

_____

GRATITUDE PROMPT

I am grateful _____

_____ .

Meet the Day

MORNING AFFIRMATION

I am steadfast and trustworthy, and I follow through on all my commitments.

MORNING GUIDED PROMPT

Reflect on a time when you allowed a situation to be as it was rather than forcing it to be something else. Celebrate your ability to accept life as it is, with gratitude.

_____

_____

_____

_____

_____

_____

_____

Rest and Reflect

EVENING AFFIRMATION

I am a good person. I am already more than enough.

WIND-DOWN PRACTICE

Self-Care Cleansing Ritual: Water

Wash away the day with water. Cleansing your face and body with water, whether it is splashing your face with water, washing your feet, or taking a full shower or bath, can be very relaxing. Washing removes the energy of the day and signals your body to relax. If you like, as you cleanse with water, try repeating this mantra in your mind: "I release the day and I welcome new beginnings." Take your time with this.

Meet the Day

AFFIRMATION GUIDANCE

We can be our own worst critics. When it comes to self-esteem, sometimes it can be helpful to see ourselves through a friend's eyes. Write an affirmation that you will say aloud to yourself while looking in the mirror.

I am _____.

How would your loved ones describe you?

_____

_____

_____

_____

_____

_____

_____

Date _____

Rest and Reflect

EVENING GUIDED PROMPT

In seeing all our commitments through, we also have a responsibility to ourselves. Knowing when to redirect our energy and effort comes from trusting our inner guidance. Recall a time when you took a different direction in life and reflect on where it led you.

_____

_____

_____

_____

_____

_____

_____

GRATITUDE PROMPT

I am grateful _____

_____.

Meet the Day

MORNING AFFIRMATION

I am ready to conquer my fears.
I will do one thing I'm scared of today.

MORNING GUIDED PROMPT

Sometimes, fear can be an opportunity to pay attention to something important. What are you inspired to try that you have previously been afraid to do?

_____

_____

_____

_____

_____

_____

_____

_____

Rest and Reflect

EVENING AFFIRMATION

I let go of limiting thoughts and beliefs.

WIND-DOWN PRACTICE

Beach Meditation for Great Sleep

This meditation is a visualization technique designed to help create a feeling of freedom and ease.

1. Find a comfortable position in a quiet space, in bed if you like.

2. Close your eyes and take 3 slow, deep breaths, inhaling and exhaling through your mouth.

3. Breathe into any physical tension and try to soften into your support.

4. Imagine yourself walking or sitting on the sand at the beach. Feel the softness between your toes and the warm sun on your skin.

5. Imagine smelling the salt air and watching the waves roll in and out.

Meet the Day

AFFIRMATION GUIDANCE

Emotions are information. Feelings of unfulfillment reveal what we don't want while feelings of joy are guides to our passions and give us direction in life.

I am passionate about _____.

How might emotion information shape your day?

_____

_____

_____

_____

_____

_____

_____

_____

_____

_____

Rest and Reflect

EVENING GUIDED PROMPT

Ayurveda teaches us that we all experience depression, anxiety, and anger at times, and that these emotions are natural aspects of elevated states. Recall a time when you experienced one of these emotions, and reflect on what you learned from the experience.

_____

_____

_____

_____

_____

_____

_____

_____

GRATITUDE PROMPT

I am grateful _____

_____.

Meet the Day

MORNING AFFIRMATION

My work is my contribution to the world.
My job is in alignment with my values.

MORNING GUIDED PROMPT

What are you currently contributing to the world in your own unique way? Why is this important to you?

_____

_____

_____

_____

_____

_____

_____

_____

Rest and Reflect

EVENING AFFIRMATION

I do my best every day to be a role model of the values I hold dear.

WIND-DOWN PRACTICE

Mantra Meditation for Better Sleep

At the end of the day, using a mantra meditation can help access our "rest and digest" nervous system response. The mantra can be anything neutral or positive.

1. Find a comfortable position, seated, reclining, or in bed.

2. Close your eyes and breathe deeply.

3. As you inhale and exhale, repeat the phrase "I am peaceful and relaxed" silently in your mind while also visualizing the words as if they were on a movie screen.

4. When your mind wanders, gently bring it back to focus on your breath and keep going.

Meet the Day

AFFIRMATION GUIDANCE

Life is an ocean of swirling emotions, with many ups and downs. We can choose to struggle against the waves of life—or we can learn to surf! We have the tools we need to navigate anything that comes our way.

I am ready for _____.

How might this inspire you in the day ahead?

_____

_____

_____

_____

_____

_____

_____

_____

Rest and Reflect

EVENING GUIDED PROMPT

What is one of your favorite ways to reward yourself, and why?

_____

_____

_____

_____

_____

_____

_____

_____

_____

GRATITUDE PROMPT

I am grateful _____

_____.

Meet the Day

MORNING AFFIRMATION

I acknowledge that what I appreciate in others also lives within myself.

MORNING GUIDED PROMPT

Think of someone who inspires you. What qualities do they exhibit that are also present within you? How are you different and unique?

_____

_____

_____

_____

_____

_____

_____

_____

Rest and Reflect

EVENING AFFIRMATION

I deserve to be loved exactly the way I want.

WIND-DOWN PRACTICE

Sweet Dreams Collage

Make a vision board for the year—without gluing or taping anything! Answer the following questions to help you put one together mentally.

1. What makes me happy?

   _____

2. What is one of my wildest dreams?

   _____

3. What is something I would like to learn?

   _____

Date

Meet the Day

AFFIRMATION GUIDANCE

Finding acceptance within ourselves begins with accepting life as it is. Everything we have experienced has brought us where we are today, which is exactly where we are supposed to be.

I am grateful to have experienced _____.

How might gratitude inspire you today?

_____

_____

_____

_____

_____

_____

_____

_____

Rest and Reflect

EVENING GUIDED PROMPT

Recall the events and feelings of the day. Did you experience self-love? Reflect on a moment when you felt confident or accomplished today.

_____

_____

_____

_____

_____

_____

_____

GRATITUDE PROMPT

I am grateful _____

_____ .

Meet the Day

MORNING AFFIRMATION

I express my joy in a way that pleases me.

MORNING GUIDED PROMPT

Imagine yourself as a successful, inspiring motivational speaker. What would you say to motivate yourself today?

_____

_____

_____

_____

_____

_____

_____

_____

Rest and Reflect

EVENING AFFIRMATION

I no longer hold myself back for fear of what others might think of me.

WIND-DOWN PRACTICE

Ho'oponopono Hawaiian Meditation for Forgiveness

Easing the energy of conflict within ourselves or with someone else can help us relax and receive the wisdom from a situation rather than holding on to the hurt and being anxious and stressed. Simply get comfortable and repeat the following mantras while breathing deeply.

1. I'm sorry.

2. Please forgive me.

3. Thank you.

4. I love you.

Close with a moment of gratitude, with your hands on your heart and a few deep breaths.

Meet the Day

AFFIRMATION GUIDANCE

Sometimes we hold ourselves back from expressing our feelings and creativity in a certain way for fear of being judged by others. What we can do instead is allow ourselves to feel the discomfort and decide we will act in a way that is authentic to us.

I am comfortable _____ .

How can you let go of your fear and express yourself a little more today?

_____

_____

_____

_____

_____

_____

_____

Rest and Reflect

EVENING GUIDED PROMPT

What styles of artistic creativity inspire you? How do you see these forms of expression within your life?

_____

_____

_____

_____

_____

_____

_____

_____

GRATITUDE PROMPT

I am grateful _____

_____.

Meet the Day

MORNING AFFIRMATION

I go with the flow of life. I release control.

MORNING GUIDED PROMPT

Surrendering to the flow of life can create a sense of ease in ourselves. Allowing ourselves to be easygoing can take a lot of stress out of life. How can you create a loose structure to give yourself some discipline without being too strict or hard on yourself?

_____

_____

_____

_____

_____

_____

_____

_____

Date

Rest and Reflect

EVENING AFFIRMATION

I release the need to control others.
I know everyone is on their own path.

WIND-DOWN PRACTICE

Body Positive Meditation

Your body is your temple, and it is one of a kind. Show some love to your body tonight.

Take a moment to look in the mirror. Take a deep breath and smile. Notice the beauty in your smile. Now regard yourself more fully. Looking back at you is a strong, smart, healthy person who deserves to be treated well. Thank your body for all it does for you.

Recall a positive moment you had with your body earlier today and write about it.

_____

_____

_____

_____

Meet the Day

AFFIRMATION GUIDANCE

Each person is entitled to their beliefs. If we can recognize that everyone is simply trying to do their best, we can celebrate our differences without feeling insecure and misunderstood.

I relinquish control of _____.

What are some things in your life you can try to accept today rather than try to control?

_____

_____

_____

_____

_____

_____

_____

_____

Rest and Reflect

EVENING GUIDED PROMPT

Implementing daily routines can help us find congruence within our bodily systems as well as in life. Even if your schedule was busy today, what rhythms did you notice that worked for you?

_____

_____

_____

_____

_____

_____

_____

_____

GRATITUDE PROMPT

I am grateful _____

_____ .

Meet the Day

MORNING AFFIRMATION

*I enjoy a healthy lifestyle because
I am committed to creating healthy habits.*

MORNING GUIDED PROMPT

Planning meals ahead of time can help us make sure we are eating delicious, healthy food. What are some favorite healthy meals or drinks you would like to make to fuel yourself today?

_____

_____

_____

_____

_____

_____

_____

Date

Rest and Reflect

EVENING AFFIRMATION

*I practice compassionate communication,
and I take nothing personally.*

WIND-DOWN PRACTICE

Insight Meditation

Insight meditation is a practice of seeing things as they really are, or continued awareness of sensation.

1. Find a comfortable seated position.

2. Take deep breaths in and out, noticing the rise and fall of the body on the inhale and exhale.

3. Notice with all your senses. Allow all sensations and stimuli to be exactly as they are. Label bodily sensations with simple words like "warmth" or "pressure."

4. When thoughts arise, label them "thinking" and continue to notice the rise and fall of the breath.

5. Continue for 5 to 7 minutes.

Meet the Day

AFFIRMATION GUIDANCE

We are all responsible for our own feelings and needs. By being honest with one another about our feelings and needs, we create clarity in communication and avoid the need for assumptions.

I am honored by honesty because _____.

What can you do today to have better communication with others?

_____

_____

_____

_____

_____

_____

_____

_____

Rest and Reflect

EVENING GUIDED PROMPT

Sometimes, we are quick to turn the blame on ourselves when our loved ones are in a funk, thinking their mood arose from something we said or did. Recall a time when you had the courage to ask how someone was feeling rather than assume you knew what they were going through.

_____

_____

_____

_____

_____

_____

_____

GRATITUDE PROMPT

I am grateful _____

_____.

Meet the Day

MORNING AFFIRMATION

I make good decisions. Every choice I make is a new opportunity for learning and growth.

MORNING GUIDED PROMPT

Reflect on a recent decision you made that was difficult, but that turned out better than you could have imagined.

_____

_____

_____

_____

_____

_____

_____

_____

Rest and Reflect

EVENING AFFIRMATION

I spend my precious time with people who bring out the best in me.

WIND-DOWN PRACTICE

Moon Gazing

Simply observing the world around us can be very calming. On a clear night, go outside and look at the moon. Ideally, have your feet on the ground, lean against a tree, or sit on the ground. Gaze at the moon, noticing what phase it is in. As you appreciate looking at the moon, take deep breaths and offer gratitude for your connection to the world. If you like, write about how gazing at the moon inspired you.

_____

_____

_____

_____

_____

Date

Meet the Day

AFFIRMATION GUIDANCE

Our adult responsibilities can weaken our connection to our inner child. But being silly and making time for play and humor is wonderful for the spirit!

I honor my inner child by _____.

How can you bring some playful energy to your day?

_____

_____

_____

_____

_____

_____

_____

_____

_____

Rest and Reflect

EVENING GUIDED PROMPT

What were some of your favorite things to do as a child? Relive and write about one of
your favorite childhood memories.

_____

_____

_____

_____

_____

_____

_____

GRATITUDE PROMPT

I am grateful _____

_____ .

Meet the Day

MORNING AFFIRMATION

I no longer overcommit myself.
I release my people-pleasing tendencies.

MORNING GUIDED PROMPT

Your time and energy are valuable. Do you have some free time built into your schedule? If not, take time now to create a schedule for the week ahead and include some open blocks of free time.

_____

_____

_____

_____

_____

_____

Date

Rest and Reflect

EVENING AFFIRMATION

I create healthy boundaries for myself.
I will say yes only when I really mean it.

WIND-DOWN PRACTICE

Dream Day Meditation

Find a comfortable position in a quiet place. Breathing deeply, imagine waking up on your perfect day. Look around—what do you notice? Where are you? Who do you see? How do you feel? What do you focus on? Imagine what you might eat for lunch. How do you spend your afternoon? How do you spend your evening? Do you attend a dinner party with friends, have a romantic dinner date, or enjoy a peaceful evening alone? If you like, write about your experience.

_____

_____

_____

_____

Meet the Day

AFFIRMATION GUIDANCE

If we are not wholeheartedly saying yes, then perhaps we should reconsider whether we really mean no. For some of us, it can be difficult to recall the last time we set boundaries and enjoyed time for ourselves.

I protect my energy by _____.

What can you do today to stay true to yourself?

_____

_____

_____

_____

_____

_____

_____

_____

Rest and Reflect

EVENING GUIDED PROMPT

Author Deepak Chopra calls the energy we feel when something is right for us "the Yum." What felt like "the Yum" for you today?

_____

_____

_____

_____

_____

_____

_____

GRATITUDE PROMPT

I am grateful _____

_____.

Meet the Day

MORNING AFFIRMATION

I clear my world of clutter and keep only what I really love.

MORNING GUIDED PROMPT

Take a few moments to imagine a space you would thrive in. What does it look like? How can you make that space a reality?

_____

_____

_____

_____

_____

_____

_____

Rest and Reflect

EVENING AFFIRMATION

*I connect with the people I love
to nurture myself and our relationship.*

WIND-DOWN PRACTICE

Connection Practice

Connection practice helps cultivate a feeling of connection with someone you care about, as well as feelings of love within yourself.

Think of someone you love—someone who makes you feel good. Imagine that person smiling and happy. What do you love about this person? How can you bring those qualities into your life? If you like, choose to write your loved one a letter. You can write it here, or on a separate piece of paper if you think you will want to send it to them later.

_____

_____

_____

_____

Meet the Day

AFFIRMATION GUIDANCE

If we divided our life into a pie, the pieces would represent major categories of life. As we change and grow, we might discover that we want something different for ourselves. We might want to add more "pieces" to our life and create something new. Consider taking some time to recognize what is important to you now.

I desire _____.

How can this desire inspire your actions today?

_____

_____

_____

_____

_____

_____

_____

_____

Rest and Reflect

EVENING GUIDED PROMPT

Recall the last time you achieved something you really wanted. Relive the excitement you felt. Why did this achievement mean so much to you?

_____

_____

_____

_____

_____

_____

_____

_____

GRATITUDE PROMPT

I am grateful _____

_____ .

Meet the Day

MORNING AFFIRMATION

I adorn my body in appreciation and in ways that feel authentic to me.

MORNING GUIDED PROMPT

When we treat our bodies well, we feel better physically, mentally, and spiritually. What is something you could do for your body every day that would enhance your life?

_____

_____

_____

_____

_____

_____

_____

_____

Rest and Reflect

EVENING AFFIRMATION

I am strong and smart.
I am in awe of my own resiliency.

WIND-DOWN PRACTICE

Third Eye Meditation for Wisdom

In some Eastern philosophies, the center of the forehead represents our inner wisdom, which is called the third eye. Try this practice to connect to your inner wisdom.

1. Settle in a comfortable, quiet place; close your eyes; and take a few deep breaths.

2. Focus your internal awareness at the forehead, between and slightly above your eyebrows.

3. Imagine a purple light in your field of vision.

4. Notice the light getting slightly brighter as you inhale, and dimmer as you exhale.

5. Set an intention to receive the wisdom of your highest self as you breathe.

6. If you like, journal about your experience.

Meet the Day

AFFIRMATION GUIDANCE

Holistic wellness includes sexual health and exploration, whether with a partner or solo. Physical touch is necessary for a human being to thrive. Our sensuality makes us feel alive!

I embrace _____.

How will you welcome in more sensuality today?

_____

_____

_____

_____

_____

_____

_____

_____

Date

Rest and Reflect

EVENING GUIDED PROMPT

You deserve some romance in your life, and it doesn't have to include a partner. Dream up a favorite date that you would give to yourself, and describe it here.

_____

_____

_____

_____

_____

_____

_____

GRATITUDE PROMPT

I am grateful _____ .

Date

Meet the Day

MORNING AFFIRMATION

I am simply amazing.

MORNING GUIDED PROMPT

Think of an activity you used to enjoy but no longer do. Do you remember why you enjoyed it? How could you bring that energy back into your life?

_____

_____

_____

_____

_____

_____

_____

_____

_____

Rest and Reflect

EVENING AFFIRMATION

I am generous and loving.
I give without attachment to the results.

WIND-DOWN PRACTICE

The Giving Tree

Think of a charitable cause you feel passionate about, and imagine the people or animals involved. Picture them gathering outside around a large tree. On the branches of the tree are things that these beings need in order to survive and be comfortable.

Now imagine this group using or consuming the "fruits" of the giving tree and how it enhances their lives. End with a moment of gratitude for all your blessings. Reflect on how you can give back to the people in your life or community.

_____

_____

_____

_____

Date

Meet the Day

AFFIRMATION GUIDANCE

The adage "give and you shall receive" holds true if we can give from a place of fulfillment rather than obligation. What we give from that place of abundance and love will show up for us in surprising ways.

I love giving _____.

What can you offer the world today that comes from your heart?

_____

_____

_____

_____

_____

_____

_____

_____

Rest and Reflect

EVENING GUIDED PROMPT

Think about the last time you volunteered for something or donated your energy and resources. What cause were you supporting, and how did it make you feel to be involved?

_____

_____

_____

_____

_____

_____

_____

_____

GRATITUDE PROMPT

I am grateful _____

_____.

Meet the Day

MORNING AFFIRMATION

Everything happens in divine timing.
I won't give up.

MORNING GUIDED PROMPT

Celebrate who you are at this time in your life by imagining your dream vacation.
How can you bring one element of that vision into your life right now?

_____

_____

_____

_____

_____

_____

_____

_____

Rest and Reflect

EVENING AFFIRMATION

I am patient and gentle with myself.

WIND-DOWN PRACTICE

Lovingkindness Mantra Meditation

Find a comfortable, supported position and close your eyes. Repeat the following words silently, and visualize them in your mind if you like.

May all beings everywhere have clean water, healthy food, and proper shelter.

May all beings be free from harm, danger, and violence of any kind.

May all beings be happy, peaceful, and free.

May my thoughts, words, and actions contribute to the good of the universe and all its inhabitants.

May there be peace on Earth, and may it begin with me.

Peace, peace, peace.

Meet the Day

AFFIRMATION GUIDANCE

It is said that when the student is ready, the teacher appears. Reflect on all the teachers you have had. Sometimes the most challenging interactions or relationships we have had in our life have been the greatest teachers. They offered gifts of wisdom we will never forget.

My wisdom comes from _____.

How might you act on this wisdom today?

_____

_____

_____

_____

_____

_____

_____

Rest and Reflect

EVENING GUIDED PROMPT

Think of a time when you called upon your patience and stayed the course in a project or relationship, and it all worked out for the best. Reflect on this memory and celebrate your faith and resilience.

_____

_____

_____

_____

_____

_____

_____

_____

GRATITUDE PROMPT

I am grateful _____

_____.

Date

Meet the Day

MORNING AFFIRMATION

I am ready to forgive and make space in my heart.

MORNING GUIDED PROMPT

Forgiving a person or situation takes courage. Accepting that everything you have experienced in your life has made you the strong person you are today, what are you now grateful for?

_____

_____

_____

_____

_____

_____

_____

Rest and Reflect

EVENING AFFIRMATION

I am grateful for my kind, gentle spirit.
I am a loving person.

WIND-DOWN PRACTICE

Nature Sounds Meditation

Time spent in nature can be very rejuvenating. There are lots of ways to bring the peace and calm of nature indoors, which can help us sleep.

Choose your favorite music streaming service and search for *nature sounds*. Pick one that feels relaxing, like the sound of gentle rain.

Get comfortable in your place of rest and listen to the sound of rain as you breathe deeply and slowly. Thank yourself for all you accomplished today, and offer gratitude. Imagine the rain washing away the day, bringing in fresh energy for tomorrow.

Date

Meet the Day

AFFIRMATION GUIDANCE

Over the course of our life, we are blessed by certain people who make us feel loved and appreciated. Love and support can enhance our lives in many ways, including increased self-esteem.

I feel love _____.

How can you infuse your day with the experience of being loved?

_____

_____

_____

_____

_____

_____

_____

_____

160 Morning & Evening Affirmation Journal

Rest and Reflect

EVENING GUIDED PROMPT

Love is an action, love is a feeling, love is a state of being. Reflect on all the ways love shows up in your life and the gratitude you feel.

_____

_____

_____

_____

_____

_____

_____

_____

GRATITUDE PROMPT

I am grateful _____

_____.

Resources

A Year of Positive Thinking: Daily Inspiration, Wisdom, and Courage by Cyndie Spiegel

Brené Brown: Check out this researcher and storyteller for wisdom on being our most authentic self. You'll find books, podcasts, TED Talks, and more.

BreneBrown.com

Chopra.com offers information on meditation, wellness, and a holistic approach to healthy living.

Chopra.com

Insight Timer is a free app that includes a timer for meditation and choices for background music, as well as hundreds of guided meditations.

InsightTimer.com

Love Yourself: 100 Empowering Affirmations to Celebrate You by Laurasia Mattingly

Soul Alchemy Course is an online group coaching course led by your author, Noelle Whittington, that helps you live a life of purpose and fulfillment. Enrollment offered seasonally.

SoulAlchemyCourse.com

References

Ackerman, Courtney E. "Gratitude Journal: A Collection of 66 Templates, Ideas, and Apps for Your Diary." PositivePsychology.com. October 22, 2021. PositivePsychology.com/gratitude-journal.

Brach, Tara. "When We Don't Make Anything 'Wrong.'" TaraBrach.com. May 28, 2012. TaraBrach.com/when-we-dont-make-anything-wrong-2-2.

Bradt, Steve. "Wandering Mind Not a Happy Mind." *The Harvard Gazette*. November 11, 2010. News.Harvard.edu/gazette/story/2010/11/wandering-mind-not-a-happy-mind.

Curry, Nancy A., and Tim Kasser. "Can Coloring Mandalas Reduce Anxiety?" *Art Therapy: Journal of the American Art Therapy Association* 22, no. 2 (2005): 81–85.

Killingsworth, Matthew A., and Daniel T. Gilbert. Supporting Online Material for "A Wandering Mind Is an Unhappy Mind." *Science* 330, no. 932 (2010). doi:10.1126/science.1192439.

Tennstedt, Sharon L., and Frederick W. Unverzagt. "The ACTIVE Study: Study Overview and Major Findings." *Journal of Aging and Health* 25, no. 8 (December 2013): 3S–20S. doi:10.1177/0898264313518133.

Friday, July 8th
- I am grateful for walks on the beach
- I am grateful for Xanax
- I am grateful sunscreen exists and is easily accessible

Saturday, July 9th
- I am grateful for good sushi
- I am grateful I started this mystery book!
- I am grateful guy asked if music too loud

Sunday, July 10th
- I am grateful this has been such perfect weather
- I am grateful Anastasia asked about registry
- I am grateful for smart TVs on vacation

163

Acknowledgments

I would like to thank my parents, Sheila Waters and Jinks Whittington, for their constant love and support. I am so grateful for their wise and steadfast guidance. I am so grateful for these special friends, teachers, and inspirations: Ashley Ludman, Girish Cruden, and Kristin Cooper Gulak. Kristin, thank you for always being there for me. Lastly, thank you to my love, Justin Heter Pan, for making life a fun, passionate, and creative adventure!

About the Author

Noelle Whittington, E-RYT 500 + YACEP, is an author, yoga mentor, life coach, and musician. Noelle is currently based in her childhood hometown of Wilmington, NC, where she teaches weekly yoga classes, is a member of several bands, and pursues solo music projects. She is the creator and founder of Soul Alchemy Course, an online group coaching course and community designed to help people find their purpose and live a life of fulfillment. She also offers music lessons, life coaching, mentorship programs for yoga teachers, and mantra and yoga philosophy studies programs both in person and online. Noelle is the senior trainer of the service-based Kunga Yoga School. Connect with Noelle on Instagram @narayanishakti and @soulalchemycourse, and learn more at Narayanishakti.com and SoulAlchemyCourse.com.

CPSIA information can be obtained
at www.ICGtesting.com
Printed in the USA
BVHW021200080222
628409BV00014B/339